I Can Be Anything!

I CAN BE

NURSE

By Nancy Greenwood

Gareth Stevens
PUBLISHING

Please visit our website, www.garethstevens.com. For a free color catalog of all our high-quality books, call toll free 1-800-542-2595 or fax 1-877-542-2596.

Library of Congress Cataloging-in-Publication Data

Names: Greenwood, Nancy, author.
Title: I can be a nurse / Nancy Greenwood.
Description: New York : Gareth Stevens Publishing, [2021] | Series: I can
  be anything! | Includes index.
Identifiers: LCCN 2019045316 | ISBN 9781538255520 (library binding) | ISBN
  9781538255506 (paperback) | ISBN 9781538255513 (6 Pack)| ISBN 9781538255537
  (ebook)
Subjects: LCSH: Nursing–Vocational guidance–Juvenile literature. |
  Nurses–Juvenile literature.
Classification: LCC RT82 .G74 2021 | DDC 610.7306/9–dc23
LC record available at https://lccn.loc.gov/2019045316

First Edition

Published in 2021 by
Gareth Stevens Publishing
111 East 14th Street, Suite 349
New York, NY 10003

Editor: Kate Mikoley
Designer: Laura Bowen

Photo credits: Cover, p. 1 (kid) StockImageFactory.com/Shutterstock.com; cover, p.1 (background) Suwin/Shutterstock.com; pp. 5 (nurse), 7, 11, 24 (nurse) Monkey Business Images/Shutterstock.com; pp. 5 (hospital), 24 (hospital) APN Photography/Shutterstock.com; pp. 9, 24 (cast) FangXiaNuo/E+/Getty Images; pp. 13, 19 Hero Images/Getty Images; p. 15 Jamie Grill/The Image Bank/Getty Images; p. 17 Ermolaev Alexander/Shutterstock.com; p. 21 Dmitry Kalinovsky/Shutterstock.com; p. 23 Jose Luis Pelaez Inc/DigitalVision/Getty Images.

Printed in the United States of America

Some of the images in this book illustrate individuals who are models. The depictions do not imply actual situations or events.

CPSIA compliance information: Batch #CS20GS: For further information contact Gareth Stevens, New York, New York at 1-800-542-2595.

Find us on

Contents

My dad is a nurse.
He works at a hospital.

He helps kids who are sick.
He makes them feel better.

Sam broke his arm.
My dad helped him
with his cast.

My dad checks
Ava's heart.
He can hear it beat!

Ms. Bow is a nurse too.
She works at my school.

I fell in the hall.
She made sure I was OK.

Tom was sick.
Ms. Bow took
his temperature.
It was high!

Nurses care for
many people.
They do lots of jobs.

Being a nurse is hard work.

I can be a nurse.
You can too!

Words to Know

cast

hospital

Index